A 30-DAY GUIDEBOOK FOR ATTRACTING
MORE LOVE, ABUNDANCE, AND
HAPPINESS INTO YOUR LIFE

JOURNAL TO
S.H.I.N.E.

JANET SCHEINER

OLD BETHPAGE, NEW YORK

For publishing inquiries, contact:
Shining Life Strategies LLC
www.janetscheiner.com

Hardcover: 979-8-9871700-1-4
Paperback: 979-8-9871700-2-1
Kindle: : 979-8-9871700-3-8

Library of Congress Cataloging Number and
Cataloging-in-Publication data on file with the publisher.

Publishing and production services by Concierge Publishing Services

Printed in the USA

10 9 8 7 6 5 4 3 2 1

DEDICATION

If you want to live a life you love, this book is dedicated to *you!* Life can be difficult and challenging at times, but when you learn to use the beautiful tools within this book, life will become amazingly different. You can journal your way to a Shining Life filled with Love, Abundance, and Happiness!

This book is also dedicated to my loving husband, Adam. Thank you for being my best friend, lover, and life partner. This journal book is my way of making the world a better place. It is my goal to help my readers to heal, align, and return to loving themselves again.

Thank you for being a part of my journey.

Janet

Butterflies are deep and powerful representations of life.
Butterflies are not only beautiful, but also have mystery,
symbolism, and meaning. They are a metaphor representing
spiritual enlightenment, transformation, change, hope, and life.

PREFACE

You are exactly where you are supposed to be right now. The things you are going through, good or bad, are the reality you've created for yourself. Thank the Universe right now for bringing you to this experience because it will help you grow, learn, and rise up to be stronger than ever before.

Your thoughts create your reality. I am going to teach you how to replace your negative thoughts with positive thoughts by focusing on everything that you are grateful for right now. You can find gratitude for everything, and you can DREAM BIG. In order for this to happen, you have to be the best version of yourself every single day. You can do this! Focus on what you want. Wake up every morning and decide, "I am going to be the best me I can be today!"

We are in this together! We are all connected. I am sending you an abundant supply of love and healing as we begin this journey together. I know our work together will help you if you are truly committed to leading a happier and more rewarding life.

CONTENTS

INTRODUCTION

My journey into journaling began when I was going through a very difficult time. I was barely surviving through my long, drawn-out divorce, and I was constantly filled with stress and worried thoughts. My children, Josh and Bari, were only 2 and 4 years old, and I worried about my future as a single mom. How would I pay my rent alone? How would I get my children off to daycare each morning? How could I arrive at work on time and show up as my very best self for my young students?

I turned to journaling each morning to vent and complain about the troubles in my life. My attention was often focused on all that was missing in my life. The pages of my journal were filled with endless problems and negativity. I was feeling overwhelmed with life, and I didn't like the person I saw in the mirror. It seemed as though I was spinning on a hamster wheel each day trying to cope with life.

I could not go on this way, and I knew something had to change

One day I decided I no longer wanted to play the victim role to the circumstances I was experiencing in my life. I'd had enough of feeling bad for myself and the cards I was dealt through my divorce.

I noticed that as I wrote down my deep thoughts and fears on paper, I always felt remarkably better. It was the first step in acknowledging their presence. This brought me one step closer to releasing my fears so I could move into a more calm and confident place.

My journal became my best friend in the morning

Setting aside five to ten minutes to write in my journal each morning was clearly changing my life.

Taking my pen to paper brought so many magical shifts.

The big changes started happening when I decided to use one of my most powerful journal techniques: "Flip the Script." I shifted the lens on my writing from a place of scarcity, lack, and fear to a place of gratitude, abundance, and love. I started paying attention to simple, small things that brought me joy, like my good health. I went on to create a longer gratitude list that included my steady job, my beautiful children, my supportive parents, the wonderful feeling of waking up rested and recharged. I thanked G-d for giving me the gift of another day here in the world to make a difference in my students' lives.

Can you guess what started happening?

The journal worked like magic, serving as an antidote to the cycle of negative emotions and worries that repeated in my head. I began to view my life in a completely different light. Flipping the script showed me that I had so many things to be thankful for. When you focus on something, it expands. The more I focused on gratitude, the more things I had to be grateful for! I went to work each day and confidently reminded myself, "Janet, you got this!"

This feeling of gratitude stayed with me throughout each day. Many of my friends even noticed that I had a much more positive attitude!

Today my journal entries reflect an empowered woman who is truly happy and confident. I love to look back through my journals and see all the challenges I courageously navigated. Retracing my journey helps me make sense of my life story so I can see all the ways I have healed my heart through writing. My journaling techniques miraculously made my life come together in ways I never could have imagined.

I am now able to get present with my emotions so I can make decisions with clarity. I have learned how to listen to my inner heart guide so I can nourish myself with inner peace each day. Journaling has helped me to rise above any limiting beliefs, doubts, worries, and fear-based stories that no longer serve me. I even manifested my best friend and soulmate by using the same journal writing techniques that I share in this book.

Most importantly, I returned to unconditionally loving myself again

I am so excited to give you a chance to experience this magic for yourself! Come along to learn how you too can leave your victim mindset behind and step into the role of "Self-Love Leader" in your life!

Are you ready? I am about to show you how to use journaling as a very important self-awareness tool to improve your life!

Welcome to the S.H.I.N.E. method of transformational journal writing.

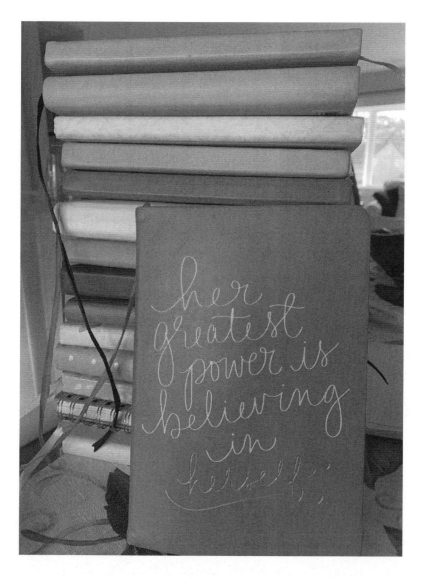

These are some of my first journals.

How Does
Journaling Work?

Wondering if I was the only human who had learned how to release negative thoughts by writing, I ended up researching my new obsession and found scientific proof of the hypotheses I had arrived at by myself. My research confirmed that journaling has tremendously positive outcomes for those who practice it consistently, including improved physical and mental health. Magic and miracles happen when you look for higher guidance and work on your own self-love and healing!

There are many scientifically proven benefits of expressive writing, particularly when it is used to process deep or stressful thoughts and feelings. Such therapeutic writing has been linked to fewer doctor visits, improved immune function, and greater mental health awareness. Writing helps you to harness the power of positive thinking to easily create a new and more desirable reality. You will feel more confident and successful in life.

To explain how journaling actually works, let's refer to the work of Dr. James Pennebaker, nationally recognized expert and author of the book *Writing to Heal*. Dr. Pennebaker affirms that "expressive writing is a very effective route to healing: emotionally, physically, and psychologically."

Dr. Pennebaker explains that there is a special relationship between the brain and the hand. When you journal regularly, your thoughts and ideas are represented in the words on your page.

Your mind is then able to process these thoughts as writing stimulates the part of the brain called the RAS—the reticular activating system. The RAS tells our brain what to focus on because we feel it is important to us. When you take the time to write down your dreams, wishes, and desires, your brain gets signals of your written goals and marks them as important. Before you know it, you're well on your way to achieving your health and life goals!

I have also studied the Law of Attraction for many years. When I watched the movie "The Secret," I was eager to learn more. The Law of Attraction recognizes that energy flows where your attention goes. In other words, you will attract into your life whatever you focus on. Journaling works very much like the Law of Attraction. When you focus on gratitude, this will allow you to attract more abundance, positive thoughts, and happiness into your life. Additionally, you will be able to manifest more joyful relationships, more money, and greater awareness.

How can you make the Law of Attraction work for you?

First, you must ASK the Universe for what you want. You can use your morning meditation to look for higher guidance and listen to your inner heart guide.

I will show you how to use your journal practice to clarify your desires and put them in motion. Do you desire a new career, new love, safe space, or a healthy and fit body? Before you can receive what you desire, you will first have to recognize what it is and then ask for it. When you are crystal clear about what you desire, you can send a powerful message to the Universe to call it in!

Second, you must truly BELIEVE that it is possible for you to fulfill your desire. You must believe that your thoughts have the power to create your reality. Use all of your senses to really feel what it will be like when you receive what you desire.

Third, you must TAKE Inspired Action toward achieving your goals and desires. Your thoughts create feelings which inspire you to take specific action. It is this Inspired Action that will bring successful results. Your actions must align with the words you speak.

Fourth, you must be prepared to RECEIVE your desires. You must become aware that you deserve happiness and abundance. Let go and trust that the Universe will deliver with perfect, divine timing. You are deserving and worthy of living a Shining Life!

I was able to manifest many good things into my own Shining Life through journaling. I found inner happiness, new cars, vacations, a new kitchen, a glowing fireplace, a lakefront Florida villa, and a wonderful husband who I absolutely adore spending time with!

After I mastered using the Law of Attraction along with writing in my journal to manifest good things in my life, I started coaching other people on developing a journal practice. Predictably, their results with my writing tools mirrored my own. That's when I knew I had to share these powerful tools more widely to help others manifest happiness too!

When I started journaling, I wished that I had a guidebook. I decided to create exactly what I had wanted: a book with all my useful journal activities to be shared and experienced. These tools and practices have helped me to feel better, increase my self-confidence, and become more present and grounded every day.

Let's Get Started!

I am so excited and passionate about sharing these techniques with you! They have worked for me in some pretty radical ways. Journaling is a process, and the tools I am going to share with you will guide you through every part of this journey as we move forward together, step by step, with me holding your hand the entire way. This book will be your companion during challenging times in your life. I am so proud of you for taking the time to strengthen your personal growth.

Where will you journal each day?

We begin by choosing a sacred journal space. The goal is to create an inviting, cozy environment for your morning practice. I invite you to find a space in your home that is quiet and peaceful so you can reflect on your feelings and dream into your future. I journal right next to a window so I can watch the sunrise and listen to the birds chirping. I encourage you to add inspiring photos, a warm cup of tea, and a glowing candle. Sitting in the same spot each day creates a healthy habit and takes the guesswork out of where you will go to write each morning.

Do you want to take your journal practice to a higher level? I always use essential oils, like Peppermint or Wild Orange, to add an energizing aroma that awakens my senses. I also keep healing crystals close by for extra support. For example, one of my favorite crystals is Citrine, the stone of abundance that carries the power of the sun. I will usually drop it into my pocket and carry it with me throughout my day.

Be sure to treat yourself to a high-quality, beautiful pen so your ideas will flow easily onto the page. Hopefully, you are getting a clear picture of how to create your own sacred journal area.

ACTION STEPS

Step 1: Walk around your home to identify and claim your sacred journal space. When you find the right spot, set up your pen and journal for the morning!

Step 2: Say the following affirmation aloud while pointing to the area you have selected: "This is my sacred journal space. It is here that I will write to find my strength and lighten my spirit! And so it is!"

MEDITATION IS EASIER THAN YOU THINK!

Meditation brings many emotional and physical benefits. It has helped me to become aware of negative thoughts and get a new perspective on stressful situations. It has also increased my patience and creativity. When you meditate, you become much more aware of your emotions. It also gets your mind off the past and into the present moment. Meditation is a simple way to reduce stress, and it takes just a few minutes!

Limiting beliefs often stop people from enjoying the many benefits of meditation. You might find yourself thinking: Am I doing this right? How can I possibly meditate when my mind is active with so many thoughts? It can be challenging to sit with your thoughts. Do not worry! With practice, meditation becomes simple and easy. You got this!

Today I will show you how to begin a basic meditation practice that you will actually love! You will find yourself looking forward to having this time alone with your thoughts, as though you are giving yourself a mini vacation sitting on the beach of a beautiful tropical island! I have spent many moments in meditation reflecting on my life and planning new goals for my future. Now you can try it yourself.

ACTION STEPS

Step 1:
Choose a comfortable, quiet place to sit. You can sit in a chair or on a blanket or cushion with your back up against a wall. Everybody is different, so find what's best for you. Allow your shoulders to relax, and place your hands gently in your lap. Close your eyes if it feels safe to do so.

Step 2:
Now bring awareness to the breath. Begin to take steady, long breaths. Notice how your breath is miraculously moving in and out of your body.

Observe the breath and energy in your body. We can learn a lot about how our bodies are feeling by observing the breath with interest. When I feel stressed, I notice that my breath is short and choppy. This is often the case at about 2 p.m. after I have been teaching all day. At this point in the day, I have probably answered 100 questions from my young, inquisitive students and made at least 300 decisions in my classroom. I often calm myself with very easy breathwork. Breathwork, the heart of a meditation practice, is the perfect tool to calm the vagus nerve—the one that controls your central nervous system. One simple type of breathwork I find to be extremely helpful is to simply inhale through your nose and then exhale slowly through pursed lips as if you are blowing through a straw.

Step 3:
Approach your meditation practice with love and acceptance. Remind yourself that you are not trying to change anything. Instead, you are breathing with curiosity. Allow yourself to

check in with your beautiful body. You can place one hand on your chest over your heart and place the other hand over your belly. As you inhale, feel your belly begin to accept more air and your chest to rise. As you exhale, draw your belly button back toward your spine, allowing the air to leave your body.

Focusing on your breath helps you to feel grounded and safe in your environment. You can return to your meditation practice anytime you feel stressed. Bringing attention to your breath will always bring you back to the present moment and away from fearful, worrisome thoughts.

It is important to realize that your mind is doing its job perfectly as it moves back and forth between thinking and doubting. When you first begin to meditate, your mind will probably be busy with your most recent to-do list! Do not get frustrated. This is completely natural. Our minds are showing us what we care for and requesting that we take care of the things on our to-do list. Your thought may be "Remember to get the dog food" because you care so much for your furry friend! It is okay; you got this! Accept your thoughts with love. Allow your thoughts to come and go and then set them aside for later. Visualize them as clouds gently passing by overhead. Trust that divine guidance will whisper messages of the utmost importance to you. As Rumi, a famous 13th-century Persian poet, reminds us, "The quieter you become, the more you are able to hear."

I am hoping you now understand how easy it is to meditate. You will learn to use your meditation practice to listen to your intuition. Every morning before you write, use this simple meditation practice before you begin. You can return to these suggestions as often as you like until you no longer need them. Meditating before journaling will soon become a healthy habit that is part of your morning routine.

LEARN TO LISTEN AND USE YOUR INTUITION

Did you know that you have your own personal inner guidance system available to help you at any time? It is called your intuition—that small, quiet voice and inner knowing inside your head.

Intuition is often referred to as a gut feeling. Your gut is lined with 100 million neurons connected to your nervous system. In many ways, your intuition is like a second brain. Do you remember the last time you had a gut feeling? Many people describe it as a sensation in their chest or stomach. It's a "knowing," or at the very least a gentle suggestion that something is off, or awesome, or needs our attention. It's a subtle whisper that doesn't clamor for your attention, which is why it's easily missed. Your intuition is always sending important messages to you.

Why is it so easy to overlook the messages from your intuition? Let's face it: We live in a very busy world. Often we do not take the time to slow down and listen.

When practiced together, meditation and journaling are powerful keys to self-awareness. When you decide to slow down and pay close attention to your body's signals, you will live a life more aligned with your unique wants, needs, and desires. You will feel more aligned, peaceful, and able to cope with the daily challenges life brings.

Through journaling, you will learn to trust your intuition, or inner heart guide, as I like to call it. I am going to show you how to connect to your intuition. Set aside five minutes in the morning to practice meditating in your sacred journal area.

ACTION STEPS

Step 1: Begin by sitting quietly in a comfortable position. Call upon your higher guidance and listen carefully.

Step 2: Explore what's coming up for you by asking yourself these questions:

> How am I feeling today?
> What do I need to learn today?
> What is life asking of me?
> What do I want to focus on today?

Step 3: Allow your pen to flow freely onto the page. Allow yourself to slow down and reflect. Continue to use these steps every day as you learn this new technique throughout the book. Meditating and tapping into your intuition will become easier with practice. Trust that your intuition is always leading you in the right direction. Keep going, you are doing great! You got this!

Step 4: Affirm your intention by saying aloud: "May I be given the power to unlock the magic of my intuition."

ARE YOU LISTENING TO YOUR EGO OR YOUR INTUITION?

As I became an expert in using the Law of Attraction with my journaling, I learned how to tell the difference between EGO and higher self. Now you can do it, too. I am going to show you how to recognize the difference between your ego voice and your intuitive voice.

Your intuitive voice will help you choose what is best for you and step into your highest self. It is always rooted in love and truth. When I fully believe that the Universe is conspiring to give me everything I desire, I know I am living in a world filled with abundance and limitless opportunities! These are my thoughts when I listen to my intuitive voice.

The messages from your ego are different from those that come from your intuition. Here are a few ways to recognize that your ego is at work:

If your thoughts are filled with fear and anxiety, you can bet you're being guided by your ego. When you feel insecure, lacking, and have a scarcity mindset, it's driven by ego. The ego voice can sound like a myriad of excuses. It is very sneaky and tricky and will do everything it needs to keep you playing small in your life and staying within your Comfort Zone.

Here's an example from my life. I wanted to go for a run outside on the nature trail near my house. My ego voice came kicking and screaming in high gear to try and stop me: *Jan, It's too hot out. You just blow dried your hair! It isn't safe on the trail. It will be getting dark soon. You can do it tomorrow.* I recognized my ego voice and went for the run anyway because I knew I would feel amazing after the run. I was right!

Intuition does not come from a place of fear. If you're feeling uplifted with ideas and thoughts from a loving, authentic place, it's your intuition whispering important messages. Always pay attention to the feelings behind the thought!

The ego dwells in the pain of the past. You have been conditioned with thoughts since you were a young child. These thoughts later become repeating stories or beliefs that you have about yourself and your life. These beliefs create the paradigm for how you operate in life. A paradigm is a program in your subconscious mind that controls your behavior and habits.

You may have the belief that your life is unfair and you are a victim of the trauma you have experienced. If you do, this message is coming from the ego voice you have been listening to for way too long!

Your newfound journaling practice will surely turn down the volume on your ego. Using my S.H.I.N.E. (Shift Higher Into New Energy) method of transformational journal writing, you will rewrite your story, revise your beliefs about your life, and live the life of a Self-Love leader.

I am going to help you shift to an exciting new paradigm for your life. As a Self-Love leader you will learn to quickly return to love whenever you are in a low vibration. Shift from barely surviving to finally thriving! This will pave the way for you to finally step into your highest self and manifest your unique Shining Life! Let's begin to Shift Higher Into New Energy together!

DAY 1

GAIN CLARITY BY USING THE LIFE HARMONY WHEEL

Gaining clarity is essential for you to achieve your life goals. If you have not had the success you want in certain areas of your life, it is most likely because you have not taken the time to get crystal clear on exactly what you desire!

Today is all about using the Life Harmony Wheel to gain clarity on what needs to be nourished in your life. I often use this tool on Sundays as a way to step back and take a bird's eye view of how my life has been going. This enables me to reflect and make any necessary changes during the next week to achieve my goals.

I was a third-grade teacher for 19 years, and then my principal decided it was time for a change. He requested I switch to being a first-grade teacher. I needed to create new lesson plans, move my classroom, and learn a new curriculum. I was feeling stressed and run down. I knew I had to make some changes in the upcoming week so I could feel my best! When I used the Life Harmony Wheel, I realized that my self-care had been neglected.

LIFE HARMONY WHEEL

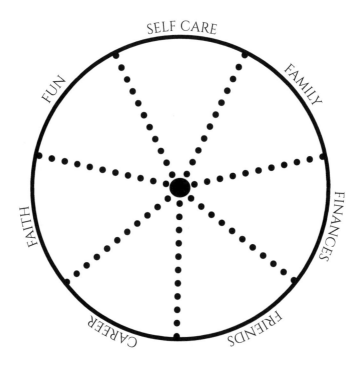

To get back on track, I mindfully planned how I could take Inspired Action to improve my self-care each day. I made a conscious effort to wear my Fitbit and track my body movement. I began to walk 10,000 steps on the nature trail daily. Making this change really helped me cope and manage my stress in a healthy way. Later I found the move to teaching first grade to be so rewarding. I encourage you to find a day each week to use the Life Harmony Wheel and check in with how you are feeling.

First, I'll show you how to tap into your intuition to gain clarity on what you truly want to manifest or improve today. Then I will show you how to align yourself by taking purposeful actions.

ACTION STEPS

Step 1: Meditate and listen carefully. When you are crystal clear about what you desire, you can send a clear message to the Universe to call it in! Remember the steps involved in using the Law of Attraction:

Ask, Believe, Take Inspired Action, and Receive.

Step 2: Take a step back and look at all the parts of your life. Go around the life harmony wheel and place a dot close to the center of the area you feel needs to be nourished. Then begin to let your pen run freely over the page. Be creative and have fun as the words spill onto the page! Add pictures or drawings if that brings you joy! Dream Big!

Get crystal clear and unapologetic about what you desire. The Universe only responds when you are sending a clear "Yes" for what you desire. Use the following questions to help guide you in identifying your desire:

◆ How do I want my future self to look and feel?
◆ What relationships in my life need improvement?
◆ Am I going through a very challenging time?
◆ Can I lean more heavily on my faith?
◆ How can I have more fun in my life?

Now that you have clarity on the area you want to improve and nourish, you will create a Return to Love Statement.

Step 3: Create a declaration of your commitment entitled "My Return to Love Statement":

I commit to improve in the area of _____.

Step 4: Say aloud, "I affirm that what I desire is on the way! Thank you!"

DAY 2

MY BIG WHY CONNECTION

Today you will set clear intentions by connecting to your Big Why! When you connect to the reasons WHY you want to fulfill your desire or improve something in your life, you will start to believe it is possible for you. This belief will propel you to move forward.

This tool is perfect for setting clear intentions. You do this by connecting to the **feelings** you will have when you attain this desire or improvement!

ACTION STEPS

Step 1: Ask yourself two questions:
How will my life be different?
How will my relationships change?

Step 2: Write in your journal:

When I _____(desire or improvement),

    I will hear _____

    I will feel _____

I will have _____

I will see _____

I will know _____

DAY 3

WORRY DUMP

This tool is a mainstay in any journaler's practice because it's such a powerful game changer. I use it almost every day because once I begin, my mind clears itself of worries so I can gain clarity on what I truly want to focus on during the rest of the day. The Worry Dump helps me let go of anxiety and depression. After my worries have been released onto the page, my mind can relax. I can later address my worries one by one, creatively identifying positive solutions.

I recommend using this tool first thing in the morning when you are just coming out of your dream state. You will find that you have the greatest access to your subconscious mind when you first wake up. The Worry Dump allows you to skim the murky pond surface from your worried mind so you can get to the clean water underneath.

This tool has dramatically improved my life by giving me greater self-awareness, since I am beginning each day with a clearer picture of my desires.

ACTION STEPS

Step 1: Dump it out. Right after you wake up, dump out anything that is on your mind! Flood the page with your thoughts, worries, ideas, and dreams.

Step 2: Connect to gratitude. With your new mental openness, write down five things you are grateful for. Connecting to gratitude is crucial because it allows your mind to focus on the good things in your life.

Step 3: Declare your deepest desires. Most of us rarely allow ourselves to actually describe our dreams aloud. If you announce to the Universe what you really want, you're placing an order for it to happen. Remember that ASK is the first step in the Law of Attraction.

Step 4: Visualize. Get extremely specific by creating stories and images of how it will feel like when you attain your desire.

Step 5: Let it go. Surrender and trust that what you are seeking is already happening on your behalf.

I hope that by now you are starting to see and feel the benefits of journaling! It is no wonder that highly successful people like Oprah and Tony Robbins begin each day with meditation and journaling.

DAY 4

BEAUTIFUL AFFIRMATIONS

Do you ever stop to notice what your thoughts are focusing on during the day?

We have more than 70,000 thoughts each day. Very often many of those thoughts are negative and filled with worries that add stress to our lives.

Remember that **you** are in charge of your thoughts and words. Your thoughts create your reality. Affirmations help me on mornings when I feel stressed and my mind is filled with negative thoughts. I am able to reframe the negative thoughts and replace them with positive ones.

As Wayne Dyer once said, "If you change the way you look at things, the things you look at change."

The two most important words in your vocabulary are "I am." Why? This is because what comes after them helps you speak your power into existence.

Focus on gratitude and the things that are going well in your life right now.

When you begin to consciously use the power of "I am" statements, your life will truly improve dramatically.

Get really clear on who you are and who you want to be! Journal your "I am" statements and declare them aloud often. When you do this, you are actually re-training your brain and conscious beliefs and speaking to your future self! You are declaring to the world your belief in who you think you are. This involves much more than just saying the words "I am confident; I am happy; I am grateful; I am successful." You have to really embody and BE the "I am" statement.

Doing this each day will change everything you experience in life. You must understand that behind every single word you say is a spell that you cast on yourself or the world around you. Words hold power because they shape your reality. You are constantly subconsciously creating your reality with the words you say.

Speak each "I am" statement with a convincing tone of voice. Feel it. Use your body language to reinforce it.

Become aware of what you say after "I am." Are you stuck in victim mode? Are you thinking that life is unfair and saying, "I am not good enough" or "I am not smart enough"? Flip the script and begin to replace these negative statements with the empowering "I am" statements of a Self-Love Leader: "I am strong enough to move mountains!" "I am smart enough to do anything I decide to do!" "I am an energetic and radiant goddess of love!"

ACTION STEPS

Step 1: Become aware of what you say after "I am."

Step 2: Replace any negative statements with more positive and loving thoughts.

Step 3: Write down your positive "I am" statements so you can revisit them whenever you need a lift.

I am _____.

I am limitless!

I am filled with love and happiness today.

I am financially abundant.

DAY 5

TWO AVATARS

This is my favorite tool to use whenever I need to release something that's been holding me back.

You are who you think you are. Sometimes the thought of taking Inspired Action can feel serious or heavy! But what if you could reframe the action to be joyful and fun? Use this tool as a motivating and powerful game that helps you shift into Self-Love Leader mode!

In this journal entry, you will create two avatars. You can playfully and creatively step into and embody the qualities of your desired avatar whenever you need to or want to, no matter what challenge you are facing!

Avatar 1: Select a fictional character or real person to symbolize yourself when you are in victim mode. It should be as much of a victim as possible, lacking motivation, passion, and energy, always making excuses.

Avatar 2: Select a role model or someone you respect and love. Pick someone you see as having the qualities you truly admire, a real Self-Love Leader!

ACTION STEPS

Step 1: Print or cut out your two avatars and place the photos in your journal. Write down the qualities and characteristics of each avatar.

Step 2: Remember that in any given moment, you have the choice to show up as Avatar 1 or 2. Decide right now that you will no longer tolerate a victim mindset. As you continue to use the journaling skills described in this book, you are powerfully stepping into the loving and abundant mindset of Avatar 2. Continue to believe that you are becoming more like that avatar every single day. One day soon, you will realize this is the new you.

DAY 6

SELF-LOVE LANGUAGE

Have you ever noticed that some people continually attract negative situations into their lives, while other people attract mostly beautiful situations?

When you start using the Law of Attraction in your journaling practice, you will have the power to shape your new reality! I am so excited to help you get rid of any self-doubt or limiting beliefs as you practice using "Self-Love Language"! You are a living, breathing, creative magnet. You can change the words you use to talk to and about yourself when you "Flip the Script."

Here's an example from my own life:

Instead of saying to myself, "I'm so scared" or "I don't know what to do" (victim language), I choose to "Flip the Script" to "Self-Love Language": "I got you, Jan. You'll figure this out easily. No worries, love. You are safe. I love you."

You will also find it very helpful to learn how to swap language like "I can't; I never; I have to; I won't" for more empowering words like "I can; I always; I get to; I will."

Start incorporating "Self-Love Language" into your daily life with the following affirmations:

I am learning to _____.

I can try to _____.

I am proud of myself for _____.

ACTION STEPS

Step 1: Meditate and listen to your self-talk. Do you sound like a critic or a cheerleader?

Step 2: Raise your awareness of how you speak to yourself throughout the day.

Step 3: Begin to reframe your self-talk by replacing negative words with more positive and self-loving thoughts. Speak to yourself like you would speak to a small child. Encourage yourself every single day and empower yourself to have confidence in your amazing abilities. *You got this!*

Step 4: Say the following affirmation aloud:

My positive thoughts create good health in my body, peace in my mind, and love in my heart.

DAY 7

FEAR LIFTER

When you are filled with fear, you really need this powerful journal tool! Fear can stop us in our tracks, especially when anxiety makes us feel stuck. The fears that plague us are the things we do not want to look at or feel, so we often overeat to fill the emptiness inside, rely on alcohol to numb our pain, or binge watch the latest trending television series to distract ourselves from our worries.

The "Fear Lifter" tool puts a mirror up to your face and guides you step by step to get clear about your fear so you can move forward with ease and grace.

Fears need to be deeply examined before they can be released. Gay Hendricks, author of *The Big Leap*, explains the importance of not falling victim to our fears and self-imposed limits. Fear is often caused by the unknown aspects of our future. Our ego tries to keep us safe by telling us to play small in life. We avoid being brave and taking risks that could help us rise up and excel.

Most of the time the fears that burden us involve issues and situations that have not yet arrived and may never even happen! Most of the issues we worry about are not even actual problems! Subconscious conditioning from our life experiences is the powerful force behind most of our fears.

Every year I get observed by my principal. This consists of a 40-minute period with him sitting in the back of my classroom typing away at his Chromebook and watching my every teaching step. When our school secretary gives me my observation date, anxiety and fear used to set in immediately. The first step in using the Fear Lifter tool is to acknowledge the fear. What exactly was causing me so much anxiety?

When I examined the fear, I remembered my favorite acronym for F.E.A.R.: False Evidence Appearing Real. I sent myself some love and reminded myself that all of the past observations from my principal had been highly positive.

I asked myself: Is it really possible that something could go wrong with my lesson? If I caught myself worrying, I worked on changing my mindset. What could I learn from this fear?

I have been teaching for 21 years now and consider myself a master teacher with valuable experience. I am always very well prepared and enjoy delivering fun and engaging lessons to my young students.

In my morning meditation, I questioned the source of my worried thoughts. I realized that the fear simply stemmed from not feeling prepared. I lifted the fear by taking Inspired Action to plan an awesome lesson for my observation. I made sure all the i's were dotted and the t's were crossed! I typed up my lesson plan and included every student question, turn and talk, detailed steps, and prepared all my materials beforehand.

When I took this Inspired Action, I felt confident and ready to deliver my rockstar lesson to the principal when he arrived at my classroom. My emotions changed from fear to excitement for my big day. I moved through the fear with the journal steps below. Now it is your turn to try using this powerful journal tool!

ACTION STEPS

Step 1: Acknowledge the fear and write it down:

The fear that is stuck in my mind is _____.

Step 2: Send it love. Feel the fear. Examine where it is coming from.

Step 3: Ask yourself if the thing you fear is really a possibility. Finding the source of your fear will help you find the solution.

Step 4: Think of an Inspired Action you can take right now to make a positive difference. Write it down.

Step 5: Say this affirmation aloud:

It is okay to feel the way I am feeling today. I am taking Inspired Action! My happiness depends on how quickly I can shift my perceptions from fear to love.

DAY 8

S.H.I.N.E. SLIDE

Are you starting to experience the benefits of journaling with me in the morning? If so, that's wonderful! The best is yet to come! Today I want to introduce you to my favorite tool, the S.H.I.N.E. Slide. S.H.I.N.E. is an acronym for Shift Higher Into New Energy. On mornings when I wake up in a funk or low vibration (feeling frustrated, edgy, or overwhelmed), I use the S.H.I.N.E. Slide journaling technique to shift toward higher-vibration feelings.

If you're wondering how feelings can be described with words like "energy" and "vibrations," please take a look at the Abraham-Hicks Emotional Guidance Scale below. The emotional scale is a list of commonly felt emotions ranging from joy, appreciation, freedom, love, and empowerment (high energy levels) to fear, despair, desperation, grief, and powerless (low energy levels).

When your emotions are low on the scale you are emitting negative energy and attracting people, situations, and experiences into your life that match that vibration. Don't

EMOTIONAL GUIDANCE SCALE

1. Joy/Appreciation/Empowerment/Freedom/Love
2. Passion
3. Enthusiasm/Eagerness/Happiness
4. Positive Expectation/Belief
5. Optimism
6. Hopefulness
7. Contentment
8. Boredom
9. Pessimism
10. Frustration/Irritation/Impatience
11. Overwhelmedness
12. Disappointment
13. Doubt
14. Worry
15. Blame
16. Discouragement
17. Anger
18. Revenge
19. Hatred/Rage
20. Jealousy
21. Insecurity/Guilt/Unworthiness
22. Fear/Grief/Desperation/Despair/Powerlessness

worry—there is something you can do! The S.H.I.N.E. Slide works exactly like a success ladder and can quickly raise your vibration and mood! You will efficiently get back into awesome alignment with your new committed role of Self-Love Leader.

The goal is to figure out where you are on the emotional scale based on your current feelings and emotions. Then you can begin to lovingly guide yourself up to joy and love.

When you lean toward joy in any situation, you will literally change the energy of everything that is happening around you! You will feel more positive, happy, peaceful, and calm.

ACTION STEPS

Step 1: Draw a lighthouse or ladder in your journal.

Step 2: Notice your current feelings or thoughts. Ask yourself, "How do I feel right now?" Write these emotions and feelings at the bottom of the lighthouse or ladder. Forgive yourself if you are feeling low-vibe emotions and just accept that this is part of being human. Send yourself some love.

Step 3: Ask for guidance or pray for more positive thoughts. Write the higher-vibration feelings you desire at the top of your lighthouse or ladder.

Step 4: Visualize yourself shifting into higher-vibration feelings. You can slide your finger from the bottom to the top of your lighthouse or ladder as you do this. (That's why I call this the S.H.I.N.E. Slide!)

DAY 9

GOAL SETTER

When a goal is written down, it is much more likely to become a reality!

Motivational speaker Tony Robbins reminds us that "Setting goals is the first step in turning the invisible into visible."

I am so excited to show you how to turn your awesome ideas into goals and then bring them into reality!

One of my favorite Law of Attraction techniques is to act "as if" I have already achieved my goal. When I was working toward my Master of Arts in Education at Queens College, I envisioned what I would be wearing, saying, and doing when I earned my degree. I visualized myself proudly walking across the stage in my sexy dress and heels with my diploma in my hand.

I also journaled in detail how I would take Inspired Action each week to earn my degree. I penciled in my daily planner the time when I would need to leave home so I could arrive in class early, get a seat in the front, and be fully present in my learning. I penciled in the times when I would meet with my study group in the library. Writing everything down helped to keep me accountable, laser focused, and on task.

When you are setting a goal for yourself, make sure it is specific and measurable. For example, the Goal Setter tool works like magic if you are desiring to lose weight.

During the winter months, I sometimes put on additional weight. With spring quickly approaching, I tried on my summer clothes and I was extremely disappointed to discover that they were tight and terribly uncomfortable. I did not like the way I looked in the mirror, and the dress material was actually cutting into my arms. I decided it was time to release the stubborn 10 pounds I had accumulated. This called for some serious goal setting! I immediately sent myself some love to completely forgive myself for gaining weight: "Don't worry, Jan. It's okay. You got this! "

Next, I used positive thinking and the power of writing in my journal to uplevel my self-discipline and commit to achieving my goal. At the top of a page in my journal, I wrote the current date and my goal of releasing 10 pounds by a specific date 60 days into the future. I also wrote my goal on an index card and tucked it into my handbag so I could read my goal card every morning when I arrived at work and remind myself how dedicated I was to losing the extra weight. I turned the goal into an affirmation: "I am so thankful and happy. I feel amazing in my spring clothes now that I'm at my slimmer goal weight."

I journaled all the details of exactly how I would take Inspired Action to reach this goal. In the process of earning my certification as a Transformational Life and Health Coach, I had learned how to create a powerful and highly effective wellness protocol for weight loss.

I created a protocol for the next 60 days. Some of the details included drinking lemon water upon rising, no snacking between meals, and no eating after 7 p.m.. I committed to walking 10,000 steps each day as recorded on my Fitbit and doing yoga to relax my nerves in the evenings.

Can you guess what happened when I reached my goal date? Of course you can! I successfully released the stubborn 10 pounds by taking Inspired Action as a Self-Love Leader! When I look in the mirror, I love the way I look and feel in my sundress. If you would like me to help you create a customized protocol for weight release, I would be very happy to help you!

I turned my idea of releasing 10 pounds into a measurable goal by writing it down in my journal. You can do the same thing for any goal that you desire to achieve. Once a goal is written, it can easily become your new reality!

Use the Goal Setter as a daily, monthly, or yearly technique. Goal setting is the essence of life! If we continue to do the same things every day, we will get the same results every day and life will become boring and dull. Setting weekly goals for myself keeps my life fresh and fun. I am always trying to grow and become a better version of myself. Achieving even the smallest goal is so rewarding and will make you a better person, parent, or professional. Now it is time for you to try it!

ACTION STEPS

Step 1: Meditate to identify a goal that you want to work toward this month.

Step 2: Connect to the reasons why this goal is very important to you. How will it change your life for the better? Visualize your high-vibration feelings after achieving this goal. See yourself taking different actions to reach your goal.

Step 3: Write your measurable, specific goal in your journal. I encourage you to highlight it and add pictures. I love to circle my goals and draw an arrow up to the very top of the page. This symbolizes my commitment to asking the Universe to support me in achieving my goal! Flag this page and review your goal daily until you reach it successfully.

Step 4: Journal the Inspired Actions you will take to achieve your goal.

Remember that it is your responsibility as a Self-Love Leader to shift your thoughts into action. You are the only one who can take charge of your life.

Before you know it, you will achieve the goal you set. You got this!

DAY 10

HEALING FREEWRITE

As a Level II Reiki energy healer, I created this technique while journaling one morning. It combines energy healing and the power of writing to heal and comfort your body.

Reiki energy creates harmony and balance in the body using powerful intentions of love. Julia Cameron, author of *Morning Pages*, explains, "Writing is a powerful form of prayer." In your practice today, you will send a prayer to heal yourself and feel better.

ACTION STEPS

Step 1: Scan your body to identify an area that needs healing. From the top of your head and down to your toes, notice if you have any tightness, soreness, or stuck energy. Where does your body feel constricted or painful? Notice how this ache feels in your system. Your body is super smart! From your head down to your throat, chest, and stomach, each place corresponds to a different chakra or energy center.

Step 2: Place your palms over the painful area. Take three long, slow breaths. Send the area loving intentions in your mind.

Write in your journal any aches or pains you are feeling. This will help you feel gratitude when the pain subsides.

Step 3: Thank the Universe or higher power for making you feel better!

DAY 11

YOUR SUPPORT SQUAD

When you're going through tough times, supportive friends and family can provide comfort and encouragement. Today's journal entry will help you create a visual reminder that will become your "go to" page whenever you are going through a difficult life change like divorce, moving to a new home, or sending your teen off to college. You can refer back to this page when you feel lonely. You will feel the comfort of being fully supported by a "Support Squad" of people who are willing and able to provide strength and encouragement. They will help you remain committed to being a Self-Love Leader.

ACTION STEPS

Step 1: Make a list of people you can always count on for support. They may be members of your faith-based community, co-workers, family members, or the members of our online community.

Step 2: Place pictures of the smiling faces of your Support Squad in your journal.

Step 3: In times of need, connect on the telephone or book a coffee date with someone special from your Support Squad. Keep them close and love them fiercely! Allow your friends to nourish and inspire you.

Step 4: Repeat the following affirmations aloud:

It is safe for me to ask for support when I need it.

I can always trust my friends and family to help me.

DAY 12

NATURE'S BEAUTY

Spending time in nature is scientifically proven to improve your mood and increase your happiness! It also reduces anxiety and enhances your immune system. Humans are designed to be outdoors. Your brain is wired to respond positively to the smells, sights, and sensations you receive outside. When I am at the beach, paying attention to my environment in a focused and mindful way feels absolutely amazing for my soul!

What are your favorite ways to enjoy time in nature? Take a break from technology and breathe in the fresh air while you soak up sunshine and Vitamin D. Take a stroll in the park or spend the day hiking on a trail.

Feeling nurtured by nature can lower your stress hormone levels! Invest in yourself by planning time on your day off or weekend to ride your bicycle with friends.

Spending a little time in nature each day goes a long way toward increasing your vitality. It helps you to become happier, healthier, and more productive.

ACTION STEPS

Step 1: Meditate and visualize all the ways you love to spend time in nature.

Step 2: In your journal, create a list of your favorite outdoor activities. To generate additional ideas, you can ask your Support Squad or family what they enjoy doing outdoors.

Step 3: Take Inspired Action and spend time outside enjoying the benefits of Mother Nature! When you are not able to go outside, think of ways to bring nature indoors. Turn your desk so you can view nature through a window. Take a mini break from work and gaze out the window to restore your energy and feel invigorated. You can also place a colorful live plant on your desk.

DAY 13

PLEASURE MENU

We live in a very busy world. Very often as we get older and gain more responsibilities, our level of pleasure diminishes. We go to work each day, care for our families, eat dinner, sleep, and repeat it all again the next day. Now and then I have to remind myself to lighten up and make time for pleasure and play. When I am having fun, I can flow through the day with more ease and grace.

As a Self-Love Leader, you are in charge of inviting more fun and joy into your life! I love to go to our local comedy club every few months with my husband, Adam. I laugh so hard my belly aches! This raises our vibration and we enjoy the positive effects of our fun evening for days afterward. After work some days, I ride my bicycle to the park. My daughter Bari and I love to swing on the swings and hang upside down on the monkey bars. We snap selfies to remember the fun memories we made together.

ACTION STEPS

Step 1: Ask yourself this question: "What have I stopped doing that I used to love doing?" Meditate on ways you could have fun and de-stress. Think back to what made you happy when you were a small child. Write in your journal to create your own unique Pleasure Menu.

Step 2: Place some of the activities from your Pleasure Menu into your calendar for the next few weeks, then take Inspired Action and go have some fun!

Step 3: Say this affirmation aloud:

Taking care of myself with activities that bring me pleasure is a radical act of love.

DAY 14

PURE GRATITUDE

An enormous amount of scientific research supports the many benefits of expressing gratitude on a daily basis. I personally have benefited from it so much that it has become a non-negotiable part of my morning routine. If I miss a day, I notice that my attitude is less optimistic and my mood is less upbeat than usual.

Nobody else can do this work for you! I strongly encourage you to consistently include expressing gratitude as part of your daily morning routine. The way you start your morning is the way you will manifest the rest of the day. I promise that you will start to see amazing results very quickly!

Gratitude has skyrocketed my life, and that is why I am so passionate about teaching you how to express gratitude as part of your journaling practice every day. This single tool, Pure Gratitude, started my whole journey with journaling to manifest my Shining Life. Pure Gratitude pulled me through a painful divorce and transformed me into a more peaceful and happy version of myself.

Gratitude shines a pipeline of light when you can't see your way out of a difficult life crisis or situation. When you focus on gratitude, you are in a place of abundance. You are not lacking anything, needing anything, or wanting anything.

Expressing gratitude connects you to the Source, Divine Love, or Universe in very much the same way that prayer does. Your inner feelings of appreciation become your manifesting magnet! When you are grateful for the good things in your life, you are sending a clear message to the Universe for more love, abundance, and happiness. The Universe will mirror back to you these high-vibration feelings and you will receive more good things than you can imagine.

Dr. Michael Beckwith reminds us, "You cannot bring anything new into your life until you are grateful for what you have now." When you begin your day by writing a list of ten things you are grateful for, you will go into your day with an attitude of pure gratitude!

ACTION STEPS

Step 1: Meditate in the morning.

Step 2: Write down at least ten things for which you are feeling appreciative right now:

I am thankful for _____.

Step 3: Sit and enjoy the feelings of happiness, harmony, and contentment that you get from reading the list that you have created. Close your eyes and bask in the high vibration of Pure Gratitude.

Writer Louise Hay says, "I have noticed that the Universe loves gratitude. The more grateful you are, the more goodies you get."

DAY 15

BEAUTY SLEEP RITUALS

M any of us lead such busy lives that we are not getting enough sleep. Does that sound like you?

Getting a good night's sleep helps you function at your best each day. When you get enough rest, you are able to concentrate more clearly and make better decisions.

Sleeping less than six hours a night is not enough! I know that when I am not well rested, I feel stressed, sluggish, edgy, and not very productive. It is also not safe to drive in this condition.

Think about how great you feel when you DO get a good night's sleep! You wake up feeling energized and ready to face the day!

Today we will focus on setting up a sleep routine that works for you! This is one of the many ways that you can truly step into the role of Self-Love Leader in your life. Bedtime is a great opportunity to nurture yourself with love.

What are some examples of bedtime rituals that can help signal your brain that it's time to wind down? You may be using some non-negotiable pre-sleep routines already. If you're looking for additional ideas, I have a few to share!

- ◆ My favorite way to wind down in the evening is with a technology power down at least two hours before bedtime.
- ◆ I always apply a few drops of lavender essential oil behind my ears and express gratitude for my day.
- ◆ Instead of eating a bedtime snack, I love to sip a hot cup of detox or lemon ginger tea after dinner. I make sure to finish the tea hours before bedtime so I am not running to the bathroom during the night!
- ◆ I treated myself to a soft fleece blanket and a pair of aloe-infused socks.
- ◆ During the winter months, I use a neck warmer before drifting off to sleep.
- ◆ In the summertime when dawn comes early, I wear an eyeshade to block the sun's rays.
- ◆ I love to listen to a prayer or soft music before falling asleep.

Bedtime is a great time to nurture yourself with self-love! Treat yourself like you would treat a brand-new baby. Take good care of yourself, just as you are always taking care of others!

Action Steps

Step 1: Think about your current routine at bedtime.

Step 2: In your journal, make a list of your non-negotiable pre-sleep rituals.

Step 3: At bedtime, say the following affirmation aloud before closing your eyes:

My mind is clear and I am ready to rest peacefully.

DAY 16

MOVEMENT MOTIVATOR

Let's get moving! We all know about the amazing health benefits of exercise, yet often we let excuses or laziness stop us from getting our much-needed daily movement. Trust me, I used to be the queen of excuses: "I'll start tomorrow." "I am too busy!" "I don't have enough time." I was always taking care of everyone else while my self-care seemed to come last.

Now that you have become a Self-Love Leader, fun movement will be a non-negotiable part of your day. To get motivated, you must tap into the reasons why you DO want to exercise! Tap into the feelings you will have after you've completed your walk or jog. I think about my body exercising, releasing unwanted toxins, experiencing the rush of endorphins flooding my brain. Once I started doing this, I started to crave exercise and truly look forward to moving each day. I even placed a picture in my journal right after I lifted weights to help me remember how fit and strong I felt at that time!

Action Steps

Step 1: Ask yourself, "How do I want to feel? How will my life change when I make exercise a non-negotiable part of my daily routine?"

Step 2: Create a list of your favorite ways to be physically active.

Step 3: Write in your journal all of your reasons for exercising and the feelings you will have after exercising.

Step 4: Revisit this journal entry whenever you need a pep talk to get outside and walk, jog, or bike! Pencil exercise into your calendar. Some other helpful ideas include creating a new music playlist, buying new sneakers, wearing a cool headband, asking a friend to join you, or consulting with a health coach for additional motivation and accountability.

Step 5: Say the following affirmation aloud:

When I move my body, I feel empowered, cleansed, and strong!

DAY 17

CLUTTER CLEARER

We can all benefit from eliminating junk that no longer brings us joy or meets our needs. Many books have been written to explain the importance of using the timeless Chinese art of *feng shui*. When we clear the clutter surrounding us, we make space to manifest more abundance and good health in our lives.

Where do you want to create abundance in your life? Will you clear your calendar to make room for a new friend or lover? May I suggest reorganizing your wallet to make space for additional cash that will soon be coming your way? Decluttering your kitchen cabinets or refrigerator will help you remove unhealthy temptations.

When I was cleaning out my bedroom closet recently, I found my favorite gorgeous dress that had become lost in the clutter.

As you are starting to realize, getting organized is an important part of self-care. Let's start with your living environment.

ACTION STEPS

Step 1: Assess the current amount of space available in each of the rooms in your home.

Step 2: Rank the rooms in regard to their importance to your well-being.

Step 3: Now it's time to get moving! Tackle one small job at a time. Eliminate unneeded items in a room, closet, drawer, or cabinet by asking yourself questions like these: Does it spark joy? Have I worn it in the past year? Consider donating unwanted clothing to your favorite worthy charity.

Step 4: Make de-cluttering fun by playing music or inviting a helpful friend!

DAY 18

"LET LOVE IN" LETTER

Do you even know how much I love you?

We often express our love for others but rarely take a moment to express some love to ourselves! Everyone needs to hear that they are doing great and to receive some encouragement to keep going! As it turns out, taking a moment for reflective journal writing brings important benefits such as decreasing anxiety and increasing your creativity and confidence. When you include some self-love, the results are even stronger. Positive messages can help you stay present, heal your heart, and increase your self-awareness.

I started writing myself love letters when I was going through my painful divorce. My ex-husband was constantly sending me lengthy, rude, hurtful emails. Each time I wrote myself a love letter, it seemed to fill my cup with love and helped me to overcome any darkness he was sending my way. I had the courage to always rise above his negative, toxic behavior and choose love and light! As my favorite mentor, Gabrielle Bernstein, often reminds me, "The Universe Always Has My Back." I am excited to share this powerful journal skill with you today so you can feel as though you too are filled with love and light!

ACTION STEPS

Step 1: Meditate. Give yourself permission to be intentional about this journal entry. Make it feel like a self-love date instead of a chore.

Step 2: Write a letter to yourself. Use "you" instead of "I" to help calm your anxiety and other intense emotions.

Here is an example:

Dear (your name),
I love how you _____.
I am proud of you for _____.

Be sure to include all the things that make you special and why you are grateful for simply BEING you! You can also write to your past self, present self, or future self.

Step 3: Thank yourself for everything you've overcome and for deciding to make positive changes in your life.

DAY 19

GROUNDING GARDEN

Does your life feel out of control at times? Journaling can help relieve stress and restore a feeling of alignment. When you are in alignment, you can fully enjoy being in the present moment of life.

How do you know when you are out of alignment? I would like to give you an example from my own life.

After a full day of teaching my first-grade students, I begin to drive home and mentally prepare to put my mom hat on. My batteries are running low and my patience is wearing thin from helping my students all day. Before stepping through the door of my house, I make sure to ground myself so I can be the best possible mom and wife for my family.

When you feel unfocused, stressed, worried, or simply depleted of energy, your body and brain are signaling that it's time for you to take a few minutes to recharge your batteries!

Here are some common ways your body lets you know that it needs a little TLC: your eyes may feel tired, your chest may feel tight, your head may ache, or your breathing may feel shallow or choppy.

When I feel this way, I stop to smell the roses with my Grounding Garden. Some of my go-to stress relief techniques include yoga, essential oils, and dancing to good music. I want to inspire you to create your own Grounding Garden to help you get back into alignment.

ACTION STEPS

Step 1: Scan your body for feelings of stress or heaviness.

Step 2: Ask yourself, "What are some ways I can reduce the stress in my life?"

Step 3: Create your own Grounding Garden! Revisit this journal entry whenever you feel the need to shift back into an aligned state of calm, peace, and focus.

Step 4: Recite the following affirmation aloud:

The more deeply I breathe, the calmer I feel.

DAY 20

FORGIVE AND LET GO

When you are cultivating self-love, the biggest key is learning how to truly forgive yourself. Learning to let go of guilt and self-blame is an important part of manifesting a Shining Life.

Here's how I use this tool in my own life. I am usually a very healthy eater. However, there have been many times when I've gone a little overboard with sweets. At times of stress, I am tempted to turn to food for comfort. When I do this, I am no longer in alignment with my health goals. Can you relate? I have learned over the years how to be a much more mindful eater.

Usually when birthday cupcakes and brownies are offered at lunch, I use my three favorite words: "No, thank you." However, every once in a while I indulge and enjoy! This is not a problem if I am making a mindful decision. However, there have been times when my will power was low and I did not make a mindful decision to have that decadent chocolate cupcake. When this happened, I used to feel guilty for self-sabotaging my healthy eating plan. I would get upset with myself, which would lead to further poor food choices. My internal dialogue sounded like this: "Well, I blew my diet, so I might as well eat this, too." I continued to sink deeper into a victim mentality and mindset! Thankfully, now if I am craving a piece of cake, I eat it and truly enjoy it! Then I move on with my life! I am thankful for my journal practice because it helps me to quickly reset to eating healthy foods that make me feel really good.

I would like to teach you the way I quickly Return to Love and let go of negative feelings such as guilt, shame, or disappointment.

We will use the ancient Hawaiian practice of Forgiveness called *"Hoʻoponopono."* This powerful healing mantra is derived from *hoʻo* (to make) and *pono* (right). It can be used at any time, and when used properly it can leave you feeling light, happy, and free. Join me as we magically follow this gentle path to true forgiveness and joy together!

ACTION STEPS

Step 1: Meditate to find out what comes up for you as something in need of your immediate attention.

Step 2: Complete the four sentences below and write them in your journal. Take responsibility and set your EGO aside as you affirm them in silence or aloud. Do whatever feels best for you. Repeat these sentences three times or until you truly feel the emotions of this healing mantra!

1. I am sorry for _____ .

2. Please forgive me for _____ .

3. Thank you for _____ .

4. I love you because _____ .

Step 3: You can sing the four sentences. You can also dance and move your beautiful body in front of the mirror while you affirm the powerful healing mantras of *Ho'oponopono!* Feel thankful for your journal practice today, as I am sure you will find this tool has truly lightened your spirit.

DAY 21

GIVING TO THE WORLD

Giving to the world is a sure way to spark more joy in your life! When we step out into service for others with a kind and helpful heart, we raise the vibration of our planet and make the world a better place.

Look for opportunities to be helpful during your day. Giving freely and joyfully is a powerful element in the manifestation process. Helping others always feels good and takes your focus off yourself and onto how you can help others.

When I wrote this book, my intention was to empower as many women as possible! Perhaps one day you will write your own book and share your personal story to inspire others.

ACTION STEPS

Step 1: Meditate and ask yourself these questions:

How can I offer my help today?

Who may need my help today?

Step 2: Write down three ideas you come up with.

Step 3: Celebrate your wins! Feel the benefit of this tool as you strengthen your sense of purpose in the world.

Step 4: Say the following affirmation aloud:

I send a prayer of love to anyone in need of a miracle today!

DAY 22

CONFIDENCE BOOSTER

I love this tool because it's such a great way to increase your self-esteem. You have to believe in yourself! I believe in you!

Research has repeatedly shown that the more you acknowledge your past successes, the more likely you will be to take on new challenges and accomplish your goals.

ACTION STEPS

Step 1: Ask yourself, "What is unique, magical, and abundant about me and my life right this very second?"

Step 2: Create a victory log to focus on your achievements. In your journal, make a list of your top three major successes in life.

I am celebrating myself for:

1.

2.

3.

Step 3: Revisit this journal page and keep expanding your list as you set new goals and accomplish them!

Step 4: Say the following affirmation aloud:

I am a confident and powerful Self-Love Leader!

DAY 23

ENERGY PROTECTOR

Everything is made up of energy, including you! Today's journaling tool will help you become more aware of your energy levels so you can truly live your life as a Self-Love Leader.

How do you know when it's time to replenish your energy? When I've been working too hard and not taking enough time for myself, I sometimes feel like I am coming down with a cold.

Although I have always been thankful to be a teacher, often by the time I say goodbye to my students at 3:30 p.m. I am physically and mentally exhausted. In addition to helping my students excel, I am responsible for replying to emails from concerned parents, making sure my lesson plans include all of the required curriculum, attending meetings with administrators, and collaborating with colleagues who have many different types of personalities.

When my children were young, I used to spend many hours driving them to after-school activities. As a divorced single mom, I knew something had to change before I became burned out. I had to get really honest with myself and find ways to balance my life by including calming self-care each day.

I asked myself, "What is no longer serving me?" Some of my other energy drainers included late-night pizza, alcohol, worrying, comparing myself to others by scrolling through Facebook, and reading upsetting emails from my ex-husband. I often tried to comfort myself with external fixes like shopping, thinking of it as "retail therapy."

These types of lower-vibration activities never improved my energy levels. Instead, they only made me feel worse. When I realized this, it was a game changer for me. I became very mindful of how I was spending my hours and days. I began replacing energy drainers with activities that brought good vibrations and made my heart happy. This journal entry will be your needed reminder to do the things that light you up and make you happy!

Whenever I begin to feel exhausted or overwhelmed, I give myself permission to take a break with a Mental Health Day. I make sure to plan the day so it will include plenty of rest and soothing spa-like activities.

Knowing that nature offers many healing benefits, I often spend time enjoying the outdoors to replenish my energy! After work, I ride my bicycle and admire the green trees and smell the beautiful aroma of fresh flowers.

The greatest benefit of this journaling tool is that it helps you notice when you are feeling drained and take Inspired Action to protect your energy!

ACTION STEPS

Step 1: Raise your awareness by taking time in the morning to get honest with yourself. Ask yourself, "What specifically is draining my energy?"

Step 2: Make a list of activities that fully replenish your energy, such as meditating, drinking lemon water, napping, taking a long nature walk, painting, or listening to high-vibe music on your way to work.

Step 3: Pencil into your planner an exact time to take Inspired Action to replenish your batteries!

DAY 24

GREAT EXPECTATIONS

This is one of my favorite manifesting tools! Many times this skill has lifted me out of the winter blues or any other funky bad mood I was feeling.

When you create a vivid mental picture of the events and good times that are coming up, you will feel more excited and optimistic about the days ahead. Remember that you have the power to control what you attract into your life.

When I was feeling dreary during a long, cold winter, I focused on my upcoming vacation and a joyful event that I would soon be attending. I imagined myself in my red bathing suit on the beach in Florida. I saw myself wearing my favorite sexy black dress to my friend's wedding in a few weeks.

In addition to looking forward to upcoming events, I make sure to stay open to welcoming something great into my life in the near future.

My favorite example of using this tool was when I manifested my wonderful husband, Adam. For several weeks before I met him, I journaled about all the specific qualities and characteristics I was hoping to find in my soul mate. I visualized how I wanted to feel around him and how my life would look with him in it. Once I expressed my clear intentions in a direct message, I surrendered to the fact that the Universe has my back, and I stepped back and let it work its magic! Voila!

Now it's your turn to try manifesting good things into your life.

Action Steps

Step 1: Ask yourself this question:

What am I looking forward to, and how do I want to feel?

Step 2: Close your eyes and visualize yourself where you want to be!

Step 3: Ask yourself this question:

What action can I take now to help me feel the way I want to feel?

Step 4: Say the following affirmation aloud:

I am grateful for all that I have in my life and for all that is coming my way!

DAY 25

"RETURN TO LOVE" MEAL COMPANION

When I was expecting my son Josh, I gained a total of 53 pounds. Soon after he was born, I decided to change my eating habits so I could return to a healthier weight. To accomplish my goal, I joined Weight Watchers and attended weekly weigh-ins and inspiring meetings.

Weight Watchers emphasizes the importance of tracking food intake when you are trying to lose weight. Each week I received a paper tracker. That's when my light bulb idea came about! I decided to use my powerful journaling practice to manifest my healthy new lighter body. Week by week, pound by pound, I used my journal as a meal companion. Today I will show you how to do this to achieve your health goals.

Be sure to select foods that nourish your soul and make you feel healthy and loved! I always start my morning with a warm cup of matcha green tea and lemon water. I love to enjoy a green smoothie for breakfast on my way to work.

How you start your morning determines how the rest of your day will go. Consciously choosing healthy foods that you truly enjoy will raise your vibration level! What will make your unique and amazing body feel good today? How about a comforting bowl of warm oatmeal with blueberries, or possibly scrambled eggs with avocado on toast?

Use this tool to get very creative with your tracking. Be sure to write down all of your foods, feelings, hunger levels, water, and movement each day. This Return to Love Meal Companion will help you to become more intentional with your eating habits.

Action Steps

Step 1: Meditate and visualize exactly how your body will look and feel when you have attained your goal.

Step 2: Write today's date and your current weight at the top of your journal page.

Step 3: Write your goal weight and underline it. Add your estimated goal achievement date.

Step 4: Write B (breakfast), L (lunch), and D (dinner) to track your meals. I also write down the time when I eat the last bite of food for the day. I remind myself, "Eating shall resume tomorrow!"

DAY 26

COMFORT ZONE STRETCHER

We spend most of our days living inside our Comfort Zone. Coming out of it can feel scary and hard! The EGO starts kicking and screaming to keep you safe.

If you want to produce different results, you must do new and scary things! You must push through the fear, because nothing will change until something changes! Many good things in life are found outside your Comfort Zone.

In order to manifest your Shining Life, you first must get rid of the "poor me" victim mindset. Let go of the feeling that there is a dark cloud hanging over your head. It is time to get your heart and mind in the right place!

The Universe will work with you if you believe great things are possible for you! Most people are afraid to believe beyond what they can see. Instead, they stick to living in their past. Allow yourself to DREAM BIG! Take that leap and believe beyond what you can see.

When you begin to stretch beyond your Comfort Zone, that's when big magic happens! You learn and grow! You become more confident and step into your power. Your Comfort Zone expands until these new things actually start to feel comfortable for you!

To stretch beyond your Comfort Zone, you will need to start doing different things that are not part of your normal routine. The trick is to expand your Comfort Zone SLOWLY with small and subtle healthy shifts!

Make sure you are not comparing yourself against others. Instead, compare your today against your yesterday. Try to improve your health by 1% each beautiful day you spend here on Earth. Today we will explore things you can do to stretch beyond the boundaries of your Comfort Zone.

ACTION STEPS

Step 1: Ask yourself, "How can I try something new or better today?"

Step 2: Challenge yourself to stretch beyond your Comfort Zone in specific ways. Here are a few ideas:

Pick up your pace while walking.

Add extra weights to your workout.

Make a change in your eating habits.

Try wearing different and exciting clothing to boost your confidence.

Step 3: Ask yourself, "What feels challenging and exciting?"

Complete the following sentence:

Something new that I truly want to accomplish is _____.

Pencil it into your calendar. After you do it, be sure to celebrate yourself for stretching beyond your Comfort Zone!

DAY 27

NEW MOON MANIFESTER

Let me start off by saying that I am by no means even close to being an astrologer! However, I have established a fun relationship with all things spiritual and a little woo!

The full moon is an ideal time to take action on the intentions you set during the new moon. Tune into the lunar cycle to plan ahead and use this amazing tool.

This is a good time to switch up the sacred space that you created. Think about adding new items to help you focus your attention inward. Suggested items include crystals, pretty photos, and affirmation cards. You can use clear quartz, the crystal for clarity, to amplify your intentions and adorn your sacred space.

Manifesting is strongest within the first eight hours following a new moon.

This is the prime time to focus your attention with great clarity on exactly what you want to manifest, create, or bring into your life. The New Moon Manifester harnesses the power of the new moon and boosts your manifesting abilities to a whole new level!

Did you know that you are constantly manifesting with your thoughts? Often we are unconsciously creating a reality we don't want by worrying, so that's what is reflected back to us! We all have the power to S.H.I.N.E. (Shift Higher Into New Energy). When you raise the vibration of your thoughts, you will attract more of what you truly desire into your life.

When you journal with the new moon, you can start to attract whatever you want in life: better health, a stronger and more loving romantic relationship, greater abundance, increased wealth. I used this tool to welcome my new husband into my life. I also used it to get a new fireplace in my home and a new car!

Create your own new moon journal activation!

This powerful ceremony begins by cleansing your sacred space of any negative or stagnant energy.

I love to burn fragrant palo santo or cleansing sage while affirming the following mantra: "I release anything that no longer serves me, and I welcome joy, love, and abundance into my life."

Use the action steps below to create your own full moon intentions. Visualize these intentions and how they will look in your life. Stay open to receiving all of your choices. The Universe provides endless opportunities. You are worthy and deserving of everything you desire!

Action Steps

Step 1: Meditate to create a clear wish list of what you want to manifest. Write down, with specific details, each of your hopes, wishes, and desires.

Step 2: Add photos or magazine images to create a mini vision board right in your journal!

Step 3: Close your eyes and enjoy the feeling of having what you want to manifest. These images should make you come alive and excite you!

Step 4: Anchor your journal page by placing one word or feeling at the center. Some suggested words are *strong, confident, calm,* and *safe.* Around your anchor word, you can add sentences like these:

I let go of _____ that is holding me back.

I invite _____ into my life.

Step 5: Once your manifesting page is laid out, completely let go. Trust that the Universe will deliver it to you with perfect divine timing. Revisit the page any time you need a jolt of inspiration!

DAY 28

MONEY MANIFESTER

Let's face it: money makes the world go around. However, money can be a tricky topic. Today I will show you how I transformed my relationship with money from a scarcity mindset to one of abundance with ease and grace!

Everything is made of energy. Money is energy that is constantly flowing in and out of your life. Your attitude about money directly affects how easily it flows to you! We often have stories and conditioning that blocks us from receiving money. This is when the Money Manifester journal entry can magically restore your faith and belief around having an abundance of money in your life!

Using the power of your pen along with the Law of Attraction, you can easily enhance your financial future. When you reframe your thoughts, you can break through old barriers and create a new Shining Life!

Remember that your thoughts create your reality. The first step is to raise your awareness around your current relationship with money. Together we will give the money in our life some love and attention. What we focus on expands. Manifesting money works very quickly when you get into the flow.

ACTION STEPS

Step 1: Meditate and envision your abundant and high-vibration life!

Step 2: In your journal, write about your current relationship with money. What was your money story growing up? What is the purpose of having money in your life? What are your fears around having too much or too little money? Dig deep to uncover your beliefs around money.

Step 3: Begin to transform your money mindset by taking Inspired Action today. What is one thing you could do today to improve your financial life?

A few years ago, I decided that Sunday would be the one day I committed to checking on my banking. I put a reminder in my phone to alert me every Sunday morning and labeled it Abundance Day! Every Sunday I make sure my accounts are all in good standing and balanced. I also express Pure Gratitude for the abundance in my life. When we express gratitude, the Universe always delivers us more things to be thankful for!

Step 4: Think about your unique talents and gifts. Perhaps one day you will share your amazing gifts with the world and create a course or book to teach and help others. I am absolutely thrilled to be sharing my gift of transformational journal writing with you today in this book. Consider joining me for a Money Manifesting Workshop where we will take our money mindset to higher levels of abundance! We will practice creative visualization and use this journal entry to create a magical vision board! We can always encounter new opportunities to manifest more money in our lives. The possibilities are simply limitless!

Step 5: Say the following affirmation aloud:

I am a successful money manifester! I am filled with abundance, wealth, and prosperity. Thank you. Thank you. Thank you!

DAY 29

SOULMATE CONNECTION

Self-love is the highest frequency of energy you can transmit. It is a powerful force that attracts everything you desire. Once you tap into this frequency, you can begin to find your soulmate. This person may be a passionate lover or a friendly companion. It is important to realize that each person desires a unique life partner, and that is perfectly fine! You are worthy of love, and it is your birthright! Manifesting and experiencing a loving relationship is only possible when you fully and deeply love yourself. When you love your life, you become a powerful attractor for a perfect match in a loving relationship.

I am absolutely certain that I manifested my husband through the Law of Attraction and journal writing. This is why I am so passionate about teaching others to use my S.H.I.N.E. method of transformational journal writing. Now I am going to share with you exactly how I did this. I will take you back to the time when I met my husband.

Since I had been working diligently to improve my self-love, I was very cautious about who I would allow into my life. I was feeling healthy and happy and taking good care of my body and mind. Self-care was key for becoming a vibrational match for my life partner!

I meditated daily and envisioned the type of soulmate I desired to come and share my life with me. I journaled the exact qualities and characteristics I was looking for in my partner. Quite honestly, I was describing the exact opposite of my ex-husband! My favorite spiritual teacher and author, Gabrielle Bernstein, often says that relationships are our greatest assignments for personal growth. Obstacles and challenges we encounter turn out to be our biggest life lessons. I had already learned the type of person that did not work for me. Fortunately for me, I was now getting a chance to choose more carefully.

I closed my eyes and held a beautiful loving vision for my soul-mate. I desired someone who would be deeply connected to his faith, timely, reliable, financially responsible, sexy, loving, fun, friendly, smart, loyal, honest, hard-working, and generous. My ideal partner would love the beach and outdoors, enjoy travel-ing, and prioritize staying physically fit. I also wanted a part-ner who would be a good role model for my children, Josh and Bari, who were 2 and 4 when I got divorced. I wrote all of this joyfully into my journal as I was specifically calling in the love I wanted to manifest. I was very mindful to send a clear mes-sage of my intentions to the Universe!

How you feel about manifesting your partner fuels the positive energy in this important message you send to the Universe. Your positive energy and thoughts will create an electromag-netic conductor for love. I am a kind, good-hearted person, and I truly believed I was worthy of finding love!

You must be open and flexible to the way your soulmate will come into your life. I met my husband one rainy Friday night in our temple. When I left my apartment that night, I was certainly not expecting to meet my wonderful husband. I was going there to pray for strength to carry on as a single working mom during a difficult time in my life. This is why I encourage you to be open to the unique way your soulmate may fall into your life!

I suggest that you try new things like taking a new route to work. You will open new dimensions for yourself, new opportunities, and new acquaintances. When my husband came to my temple that Friday night, it was his first time there. He was searching for a new temple and coincidentally decided to try the one I had been frequently attending.

Today we have been happily married for ten years. We laugh often as we finish each other's sentences. I feel as though I was meant to spend my life with him. In the Jewish culture, we say he is my *beshert*. We enjoy going to the beach together, jogging alongside each other on the nature trail, and of course going every Friday night to the temple where we met. We are so thankful that we are truly enjoying our lives together! The reason I share this with you is to reiterate the importance of setting a clear intention of the soulmate you would love to share your life with. Never settle for mediocrity. As a Self-Love Leader, it is your responsibility to advocate for yourself and specifically call in the passionate love you desire!

I hope my story gives you hope that you will meet your soulmate! And if you have already found your soulmate, I hope my story will increase your appreciation for the love you share!

ACTION STEPS

Step 1: Get into perfect alignment. Shake off any negative vibes. Fuel your positive attitude with high-vibe thoughts. Believe you are worthy and deserving to meet your soulmate. Light a candle and play some romantic music as you prepare to journal. This will truly help you to become a vibrational match for your partner!

Step 2: Engage your mind, body, and spirit with today's writing. Describe where you picture yourself meeting your soulmate. Close your eyes and use your imagination to set a crystal-clear intention. Open your arms, stand up tall and expand your chest, and look upward with a gentle smile of appreciation. Breathe deeply in and out.

Step 3: Write down specific things you want in your partner. How do they make you feel? How do you feel around them? How will your life change? What are you wearing? What will you do together? Let your heart guide you as you journal.

Step 4: Take Inspired Action! Show the Universe you are committed to this intention of finding your soulmate. Will you join an online dating service, spread the word to friends that you are open to meeting someone, or join a new gym? How can you close the gap and bring this person closer to your current life?

Step 5: Be open to receiving a loving soulmate soon. Unattach to any expectations that it will happen at a specific place and time. Feel grateful, acting "as if" your soulmate has already come into your life. Surrender and completely trust the Universe to deliver! You got this!

Step 6: Say the following affirmation aloud:

I speak my thoughts and words into action! The Universe is always conspiring to give me everything I want.

DAY 30

CELEBRATION

Congratulations! You did it! This day is the culmination and celebration of all your hard work over the last 29 days. Not only have you done the important inner work of self-development, but you are also experiencing increased joy and heightened awareness as you S.H.I.N.E. (Shift Higher Into New Energy) in your role as Self-Love Leader in your life!

Try to be the type of journaler who writes when your life is absolutely fantastic, as well as when you feel like everything is falling apart! Remember that the Law of Attraction teaches that what you focus on expands! The more you journal when things are awesome, the more you will manifest abundance and happiness in your life! Feel the richness of your bliss! Give yourself permission to feel good! Notice how you got into this high-vibe state and most important, how you can stay there and return to love any time you wander away!

You have used these 30 days to step into a new and healthier improved you, shifted into more positive energy and happiness, and created your unique Shining Life. I hope you have enjoyed this transformation and that you are feeling more connected to your inner heart guide… more peaceful, calm, focused, and positive through my S.H.I.N.E method of transformational journaling.

Take time to write in your journal about the big takeaways and powerful shifts you've noticed in your life since you started journaling with me. Share these insights with your friends and family! It has been my pleasure to guide you on this journey. I am forever grateful you decided to join me.

Are you wondering how to stay motivated and continue to experience amazing personal growth? Look back at the Life Harmony Wheel. Ask yourself, "What do I want to manifest next in my journal?" Reach out to me to book a S.H.I.N.E. session through email: shininglifehc@gmail.com.

Remember that you are able to make many choices each day of your life. You decide how you want to show up in the world. You decide what types of thoughts you want to have, what foods you will choose to nourish your body, and how you will engage your body in movement.

You have the power to show up as a Self-Love Leader in your life. Leave behind the stressed and worried victim mindset! You have the journaling tools now to listen to your intuition and take aligned and focused action. You've seen how your thoughts create your reality. You have decided to Rise Up and S.H.I.N.E. with a more positive mindset. I am so proud of you! I am sending abundant light and love to accompany you on your journey through life.

ABOUT THE AUTHOR

◆

Janet Scheiner is a certified Health & Life Coach, a Level II Reiki Practitioner, and a certified RYT 200 hour instructor for Trauma Informed Yoga and Mindfulness. She is also a first-grade teacher in the same elementary school that she attended as a child. Janet resides in Long Island, NY, and credits journaling, the Law of Attraction, and The Secret for helping her gain a sense of empowerment to Rise Up and S.H.I.N.E. through life's challenges.

Visit her at www.janetscheiner.com

Made in the USA
Middletown, DE
07 August 2023

36318795R00066